I0489714

The Potter and Sculptress

Clay – Ceramic Wheel Throwing – Hand Designs

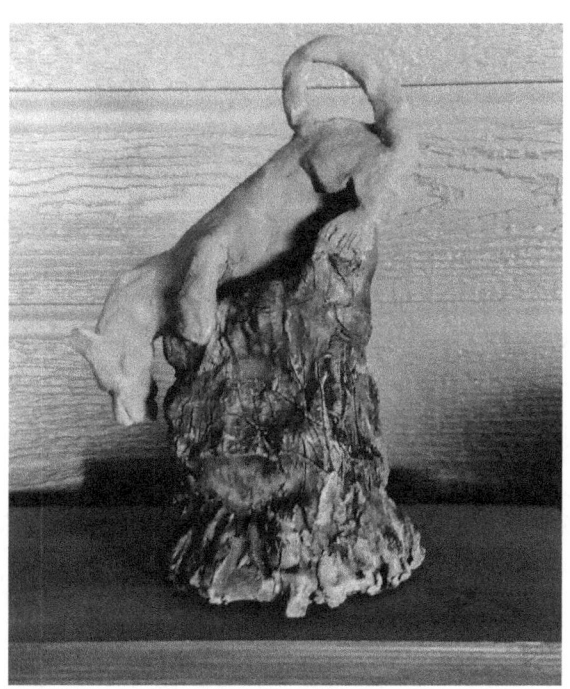

Peggy Leyva Conley

Thank you for reading. In the event that you Appreciate this book, please consider sharing the Good word(s) by leaving a review, or connect with the author.

All rights reserved. Aside from brief quotations for Media coverage and reviews, no part of this book may be reproduced or distributed in any form without the author's permission. Thank you for supporting authors and a diverse, creative culture by purchasing this book and complying with copyright laws.

Copyright © 2016 - Peggy Leyva-Conley
Pottery, Ceramics, Sculpture, Photography

All Rights Reserved

Printed in the United States of America

ISBN: 13: 978-1533002709 (Createspace) paperback
ISBN: 10: 1533002703

Dedication

To all Artist of the World
and those who appreciate the Arts
as a form of helping to
Heal humanity.

Table of Contents

Earth Galaxy Bowl
New Mexico Spice Bowls
Scottish Highlands Horse - Sculptor
Appalachian Blue Bird and Nest Eggs
Blue Bird – Sculptor
Visionary in Meditation – Sculptor
Women of Wisdom – Sculptor
Teapot and Cups
Ancient Oil Lamp
Incense Stick Holder
Santa Cruz de Rosales Nuns de Mexico - Sculptors
Tropical Turtle - Sculptor
Native American Harvest – Sculptor
Victorian Country Water Pitcher
Hat of the Sun
Sundial Disk
Pacific Starfish

About the Author

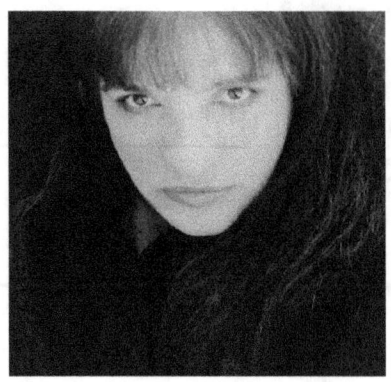

Peggy Leyva Conley was born in Hollister, California, San Benito County near the border of Monterey County.

She also has resided in Hendersonville, Tennessee a Suburb of Nashville while in the Music business. She currently resides in Rocklin, California on the bottom Basin of Tahoe National Forest near the Capitol City of Sacramento.

Educational Courses in Pottery, Ceramics and Sculptor Designing throughout years of Study, and formal training included exhibiting her work.

She received a High Honor Art Scholarship from the "San Benito Artist" in Hollister, California.

As an Artist, she has been Honored and Awarded for Artworks, and Ceramics produced throughout her Career, including showing at Galleries.

She received formal training also working at the C&C Ceramic Shop in Hollister, California under professional guidance of Certified Teachers in Pottery.

She is a Member of the National League American Pen Women-Nashville Branch (Art, Music, and Writing) affiliated with Headquarters in Washington DC and is a member of the United Poets Laureate International – United Nations.

She is an International Musician and Published Author of Music, Art, Photography, Aromatherapy, and Genealogy.

The Artist enjoys Hiking, Tennis, Plein Air Painting, Traveling and Archeology studies.

She has worked in Aerospace and Telecommunications high Tech Industry in Northern California.

She received a CMII Configuration Management Certificate in Engineering from the University of Phoenix and Sun Microsystems Technical School for System Administration with use of Solaris/Unix Programming in Computer Science located in Silicon Valley.

Shoshone Rocks and Cliffs

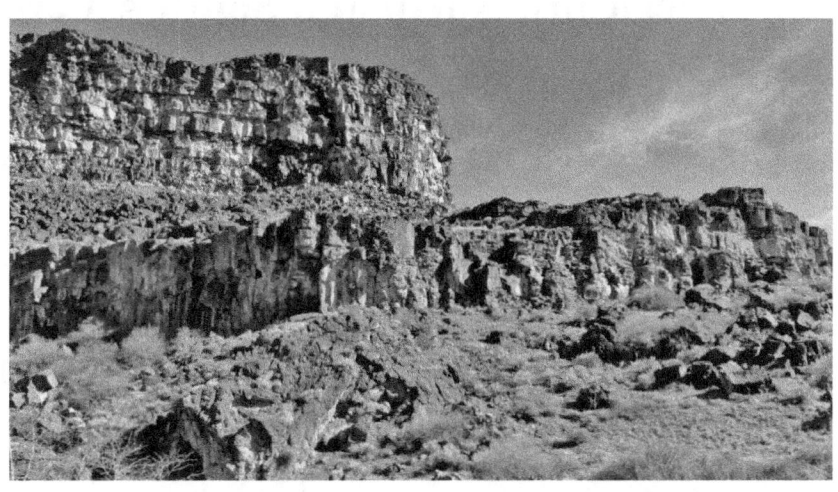

Near Twin Falls, Idaho

The Clay used in much of the United States comes from Minerals for Pottery and Ceramics throughout many parts of America.

The Canyons are examples of where Red Clay is found and are an inspiration with use of Color tones in the Art fields. The Native American Indians left traces of Pottery in North and South America found by Archeologist.

Styles and Influences

Europeans – United States
Native Americans, North and South America

In Traveling throughout parts of California, Arizona, New Mexico, Texas, Idaho and Central Chihuahua, Mexico one has seen some of the best Potters, and Sculptors due to the Native American culture. Including diverse Artist who come in from different parts of the World to reside, and retire in these Artist communities.

This includes expeditions into parts of the Appalachian Mountains in Eastern Tennessee, North Carolina, Georgia and Virginia well known for Stoneware, Pottery, and Ceramics. The Mountain Folks are often referred to as Artisans.

Many of the early European Settlers brought their Skills from England, Ireland, Germany and Holland passing on the knowledge to the younger generations in many families.

The Native American Indian Tribes have been located throughout the Nation and left behind remnants discovered by researchers throughout history of their Culture and works.

The rich Soil found in many of these States makeup for the Bags of Clay shipped around the Country from distributors for Potters to create products.

Many of the items Created in this book where originally named after some of the places the Potter and Sculptress has traveled on location, including out of Historical significance to Pottery, and Cultures.

Pottery

Lead-Free for Use

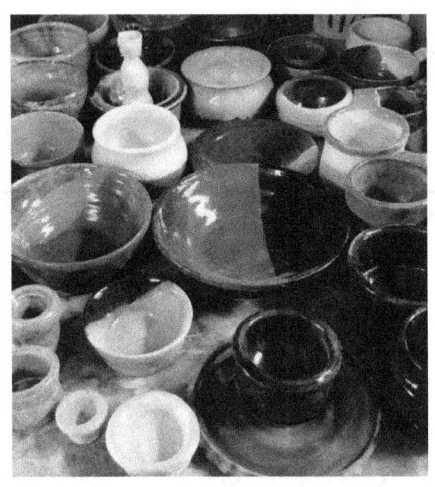

Pottery can come in many forms such as Bowls, Cups, and Saucers to produce items for use.

There are many Ceramic Paints (lead-free) to use for your products so they are safe to Cook in and drink beverages.

Always consulate a professional and read the Labels for Safety precautions to make sure before use.

Types of Pottery

Clay: Contains Minerals and have Organic matter, and amounts of Water.

Earthenware: Low-Fired Pottery.

Stoneware: Fired at high Temperatures and considered Semi-Ceramic.

Porcelain: A form of Ceramic created by heating the materials at higher temperature degrees in the Kiln.

Greenware: Clay objects requiring to be put into the Kiln for firing.

Bisque: After the Clay has been put into the Kiln for Firing, it is then referred to as Bisque.

Glaze: Used on Ceramics and requires Firing in the Kiln for products.

Ceramic Wheel Throwing

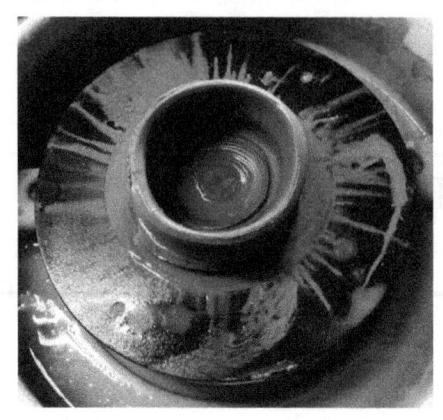

Pottery Bowl

Ceramic Wheel Throwing is a term in essence meaning to choose an amount of Clay to work with and making sure to center some onto the Wheel in order for it to stick. Then begin using the Wheel to spin while working with your Hands to design and create Pottery projects.

Use a chair to sit in and position your body centered enough to be comfortable. Make sure to have enough Water in a bowl set aside to use in working with the Clay on the Wheel.

There is a pedal on the floor to control the Wheel spinning at a slow, moderate or fast speed.

Use your hands to press down the Clay and begin working to create any style or design of Ceramic pieces made out of the Clay on the Wheel.

Types of Tools

Brushes: Used for glazing products created with brush strokes.

Ribs and Scrappers: Used to help smooth out Clay projects and help to shape them.

Wooden Modeling Tool: Used to help Trim or hand design projects created.

Chamois: Helps to smooth or compress the Ware.

Potter's Needles: Use for trimming the Ware and Scoring.

Sponges: Used to absorb excess Water on projects.

Wires: Use your left and right hand on the wooden handles, and the Wire Line to cut-off Clay projects from the Wheel carefully when removing.

Kiln: Used to put in products to Fire at low, medium or high temperatures depending on the material used such as Clay or Stoneware.

Kiln

Firing – Bisque

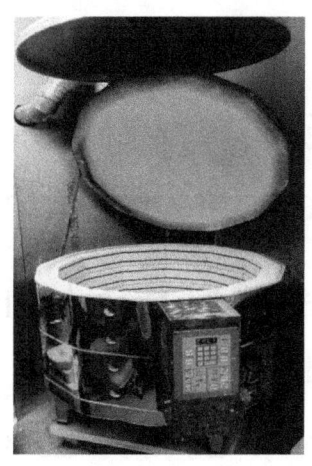

Used for Firing Greenware, Pottery, Ceramics, Stoneware and Porcelain. The Pottery then comes out as Bisque once Firing has taken place. Each project must be given time to Cool down upon completion of the Firing phase and process. This helps to keep the Pottery from exploding and breaking into pieces.

Temperature setting must be determined by the type of Clay used and Cone levels.

Paints

Low Sheen – High Gloss

Strokes and Coats of Layer

All the products originally produced in this book have been created by Hand or on the Potter's Wheel.

Each Project completed obtained one each Firing in the Kiln. It is then called Bisque once the initial Firing has occurred. The Pottery was set at various Temperatures and Cone levels for firing.

After cooling down, they were removed from the Kiln. Later four each Coats of Paint are applied with a brush to each project. This may involve Low Sheen or High Gloss Coats to give the Pottery various degrees of styles independent of one another. Then the projects where put into the Kiln for a second Firing.

Potter Wheels

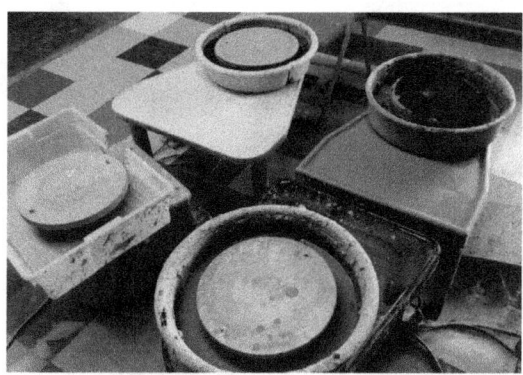

The Potter Wheels are used for creating and designing projects by hand with Clay or Stoneware, and other materials determined by the Artist.

In the Studio

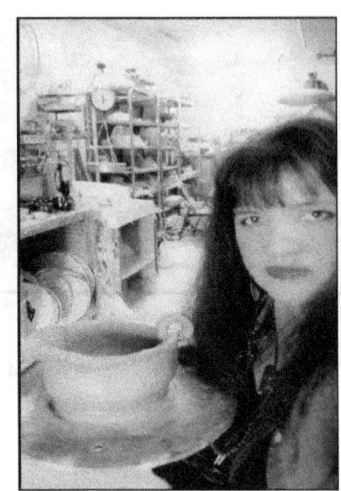

Creating a Country Water Pitcher using the Potter's Wheel on location in Historic downtown Nampa, Idaho a suburb of Boise.

The downtown area thrives on Artist, Jewelry Designers, Clothing Consignments, Book Stores, Coffee Houses, a Theater, Pubs, Fine Dining and printing houses for writers.

Virginia Cornmeal Bowl

Stoneware

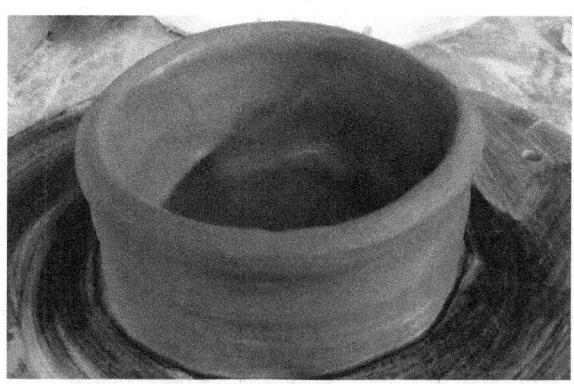

This Bowl is round and created on the Potter's Wheel using Stoneware material.

The Native American Indians used Bowls to store Cornmeal in and herbs. They are beneficial for many other uses as well.

Female Morning Stretch

Sculptor

High Gloss/Bisque

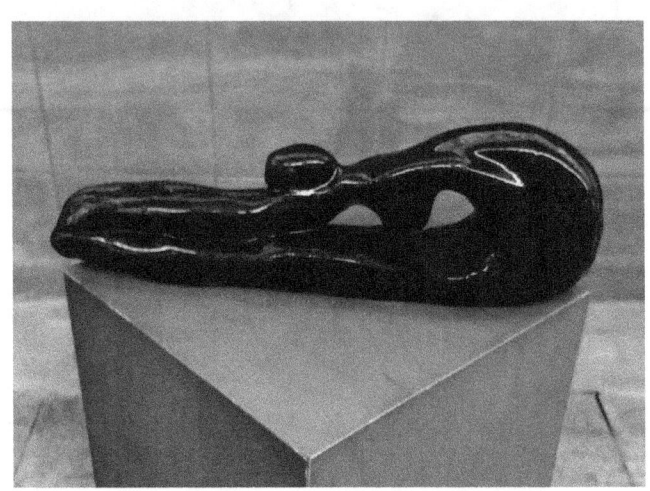

A female Body Form in Art with movement.

California Cougar

Sculptor

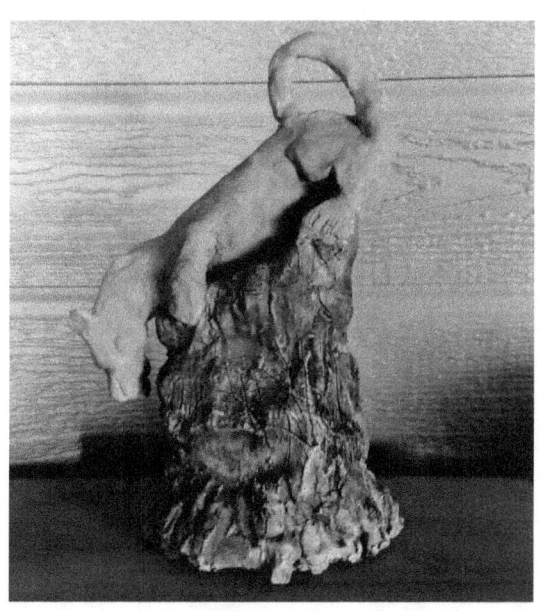

The Cougar species can be found in the Carmel, Monterey, Salinas Valley and Aromas Hillsides, as it is part of their Natural habitat. They roam most Mountain Ranges throughout various regions of California.

Albuquerque Bowl

New Mexico

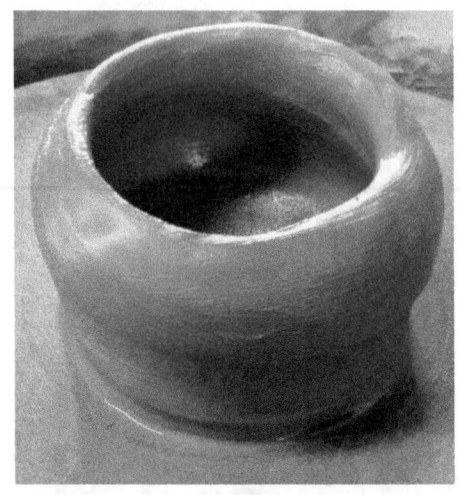

The Albuquerque, New Mexico area has been recognized for Potters and Artist.

The Clay found in the Mountains nearby were used by the Native American Indians. Archaeologist in parts of the region has studied many Artifacts.

Tennessee Tobacco Bowl

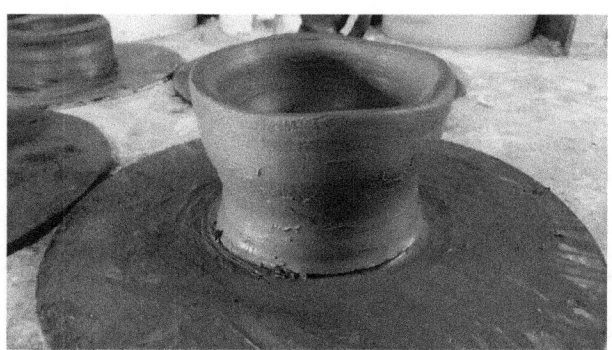

The Tobacco Bowl is used to store dried leaves in.

A Gentleman may sit with a Pipe laying next to the Bowl on a table stand. Some of the leaves would be removed with their hands to insert into the Pipe to smoke.

Men in the Colonial time-periods enjoyed Smoking while reading books accompanied at times by a shot of brandy or liqueur.

Pueblo Bowls and River Rocks

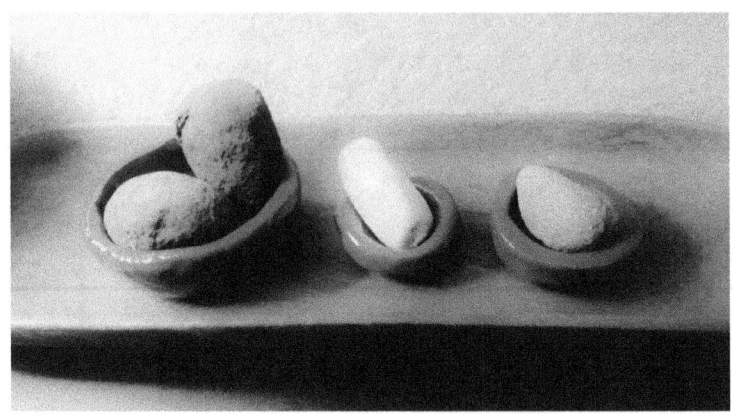

The people of many Cultures and backgrounds have used Bowls to store objects, and herbs including keepsakes.

These contain River Rocks from parts of Idaho and California.

Irish Spiral Bowl

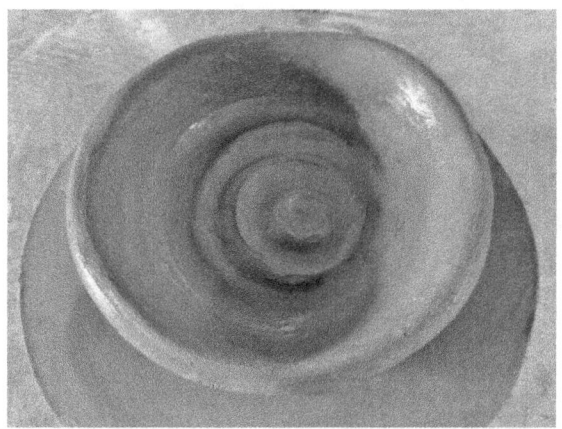

The Spiral of Life was created on some Irish stone carvings over centuries in Caves and other Cultures around the world.

Left Hand Freedom

Sculptor

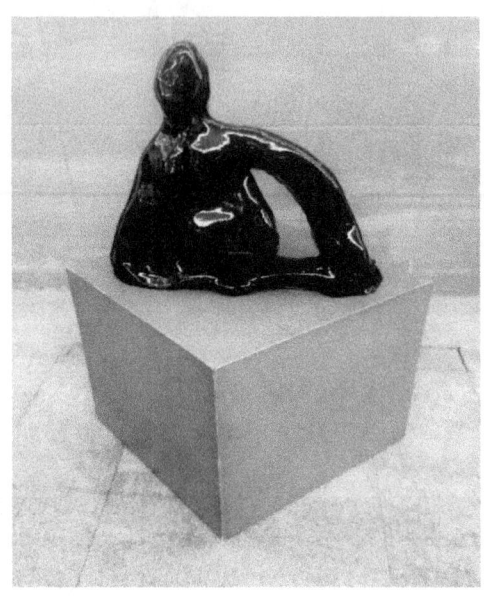

The Left Hand outward indicates the Symbolism of Freedom as Artist to create without restriction.

Copper Canyon Bowl

Chihuahua, Mexico

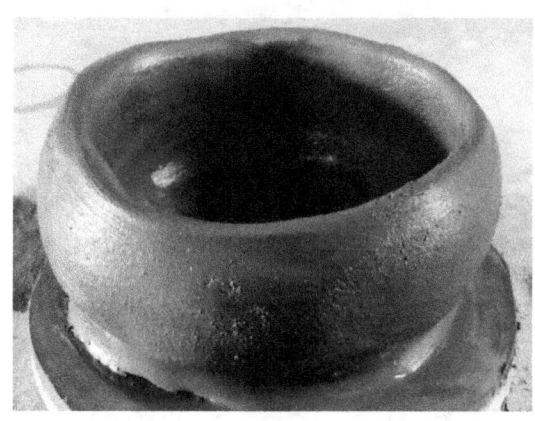

The Copper Canyon has some of the deepest areas of Rugged and Mountain Ranges. There are Rivers and Waterfalls in the Canyons.

The Tarahumara Indians reside in this part of the region. Early history indicates the Paquime civilization was here even earlier. Many travelers come to visit the area. This area has Forest, Flowers, Cactus and Wildlife species. The area was known for its Silver when the Spanish Conquistadors arrived from Spain. The crop is Corn in the region as a food source.

Arizona Nopal Cactus Drink Cup

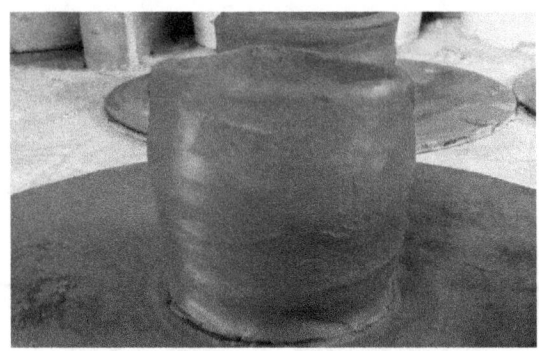

The Nopal Cactus Drink can consist of enough Orange Juice, Pineapple and one Cactus (Nopal Pad) removing the needles first.

Use a Blender and insert all the ingredients into the mixer with Ice-cubes. The Nopal Pads can be found at a Mexican Super Market. This drink is like a Smoothie and popular throughout parts of the Southwest as is the Cactus Watermelon drink in Mexico.

North Carolina Cinnamon Holder

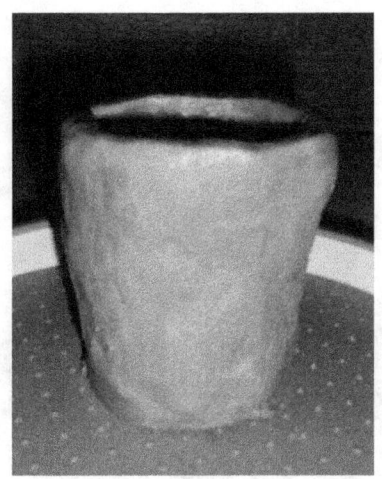

North Carolina history of Potters goes back in time among early Settlers and those of Colonial time-periods.

Many early American Potters came out of various areas as some of the best in the nation.

This is a Cinnamon holder to set aside on a Kitchen Counter for use in Cooking.

Earth Galaxy Bowl

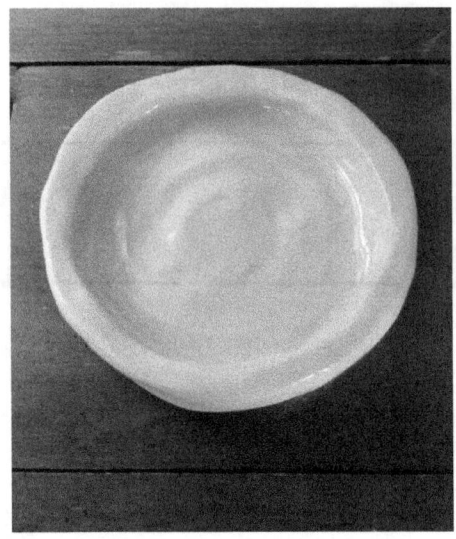

The Earth Bowl represents the Circular movement as that of the Spiral in life. The Bowl is good to store other things such as Jewelry, Rings, Bracelets and Coins.

New Mexico Spice Bowls

High Gloss Finish – Food Safe /Non-Toxic

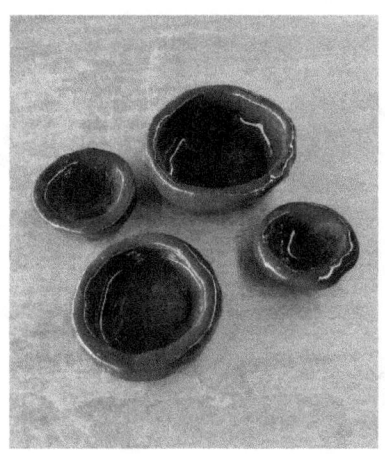

These Spice Bowls have use for containing Salt, Black pepper, Red Chili, Parsley, Oregano, Sage and Rosemary.

Scottish Highlands Horse

Sculptor

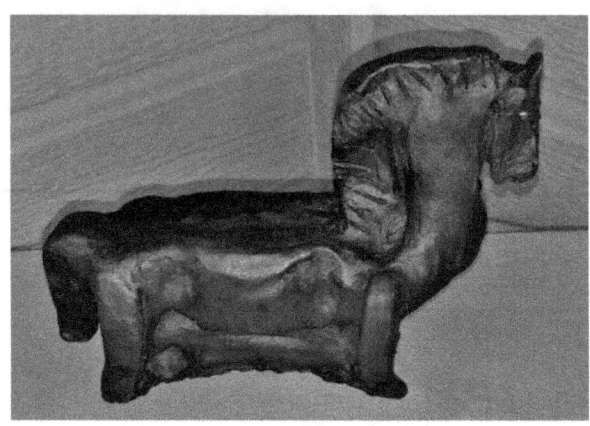

The Scottish Highlands Horse was used on Farms and for Trail riding. The area has large Mountain ranges.

The area is Scenic with Rolling Hillsides, Wooden Fences, Farms, Wildflowers and Bracken. Scotland is considered part of the British Isles.

Appalachian Blue Bird and Nest Eggs

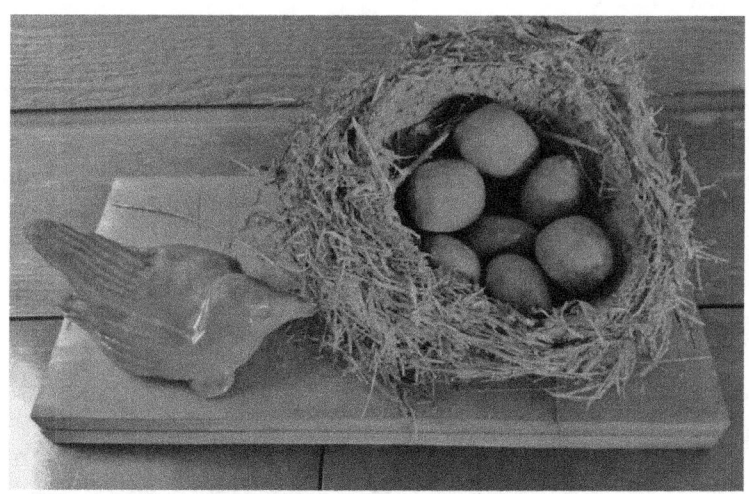

The Tazewell, Tennessee area in the Appalachian Mountains is well known for many Bird Species.

The area is pristine with Nature and beauty throughout the land. Early Pioneers have settled the area.

Blue Bird

Sculptor

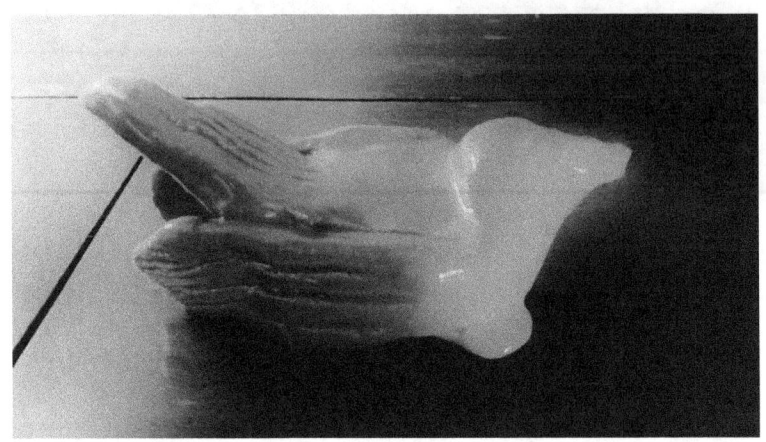

The Clay Bird was created by hand and then allowed to dry. It was then inserted into the Kiln for a First firing.

Once it was cooled down then four Coats of High Gloss Paint was added using a Paintbrush. The project was then inserted back into the Kiln for a final and second firing.

Visionary in Meditation

Sculptor

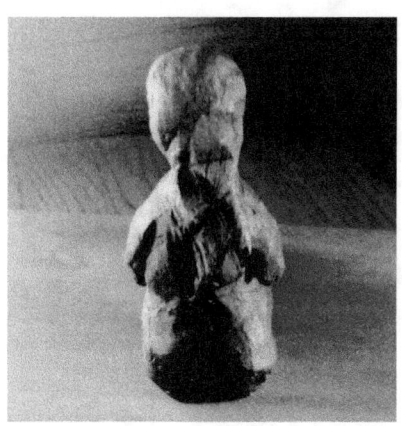

As Artist, it is essential to be centered with Harmony and Peace in life.

Meditation and learning to relax from stress is important in each individual's life for healing in the World.

Women of Wisdom

Sculptor

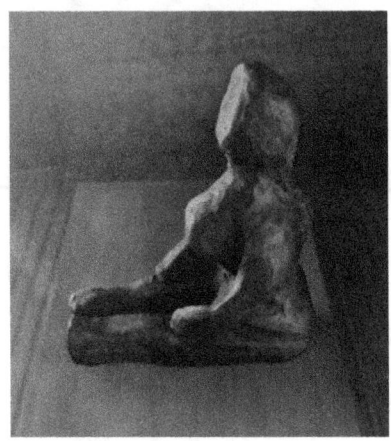

Learning to sit in one place alone and be still in the moment is important in order to hear the Calling in you.

Pray and hold Steadfast in Faith.

Teapot and Cups

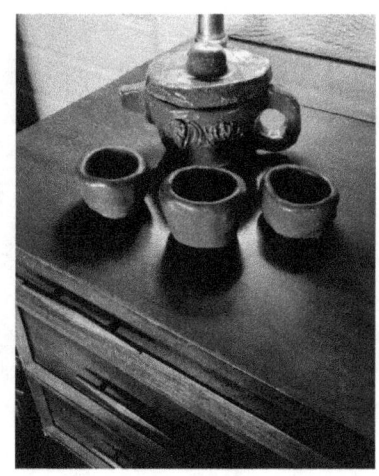

Green and Black Tea is good in the Morning for relaxing and meditating while listening to Instrumental, and healing music.

Ancient Oil Lamp

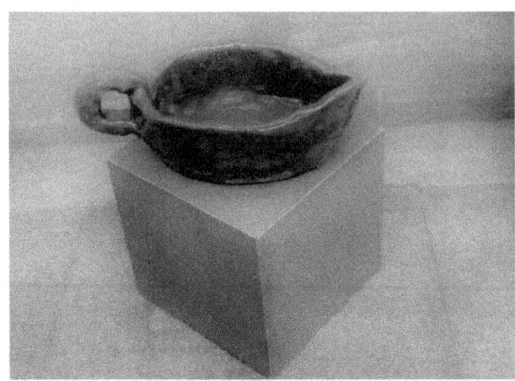

Oil Lamps where used during Ancient times. A Wick was put on the front Lip of the Lamp and Oil inserted in the dish. This kept it burning for long hours.

Incense Stick Holder

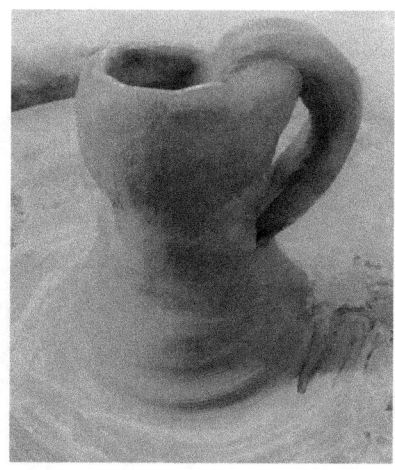

Lighting an Incense Stick brings Fragrance into a home. Some come in Rosewood, Lavender, Sandalwood and Jasmine scents.

The Sticks of Incense can be found at Exotic Shops with imports from India in places like Santa Cruz, California on the Pacific Central Coastal region.

Santa Cruz de Rosales Nuns de Mexico

Sculptors

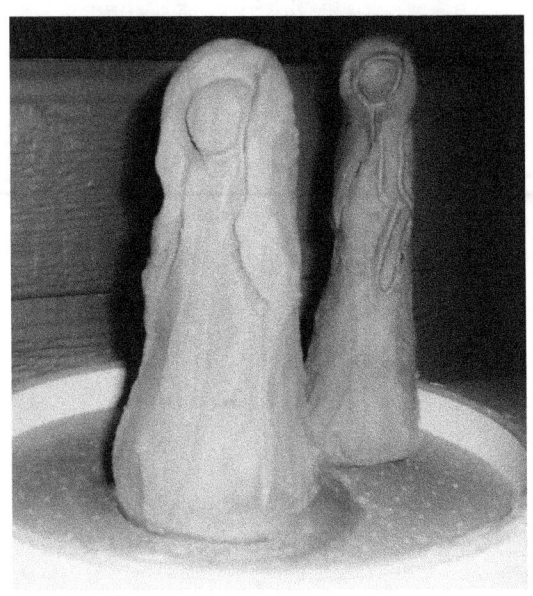

Many Nuns help children and people in need around the World by their Spiritual work, and duties.

Tropical Turtle

Sculptor

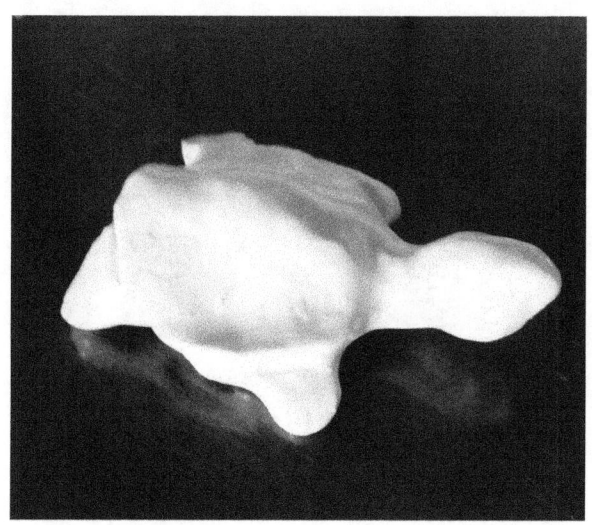

The Turtle can be found in many Tropical locations around the World.

Native American Harvest

Sculptor

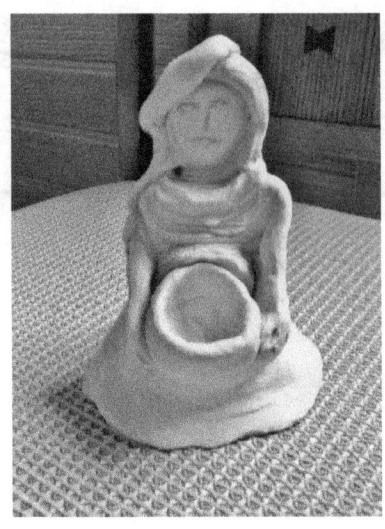

The Bowl represents the Food Harvest during the Season where Corn, Squash and Pumpkins are gathered for Celebration by the Native American Women.

Victorian Country Water Pitcher

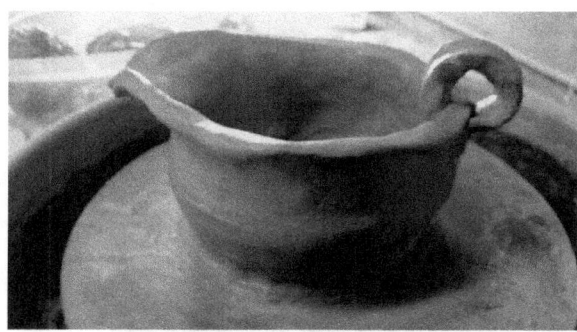

The Country Water Pitcher during the Victorian era was placed near a bowl on a dresser.

The Water would be poured into the Bowl to use in washing their face. Then they would use a Cloth towel to dry off.

Hat of the Sun

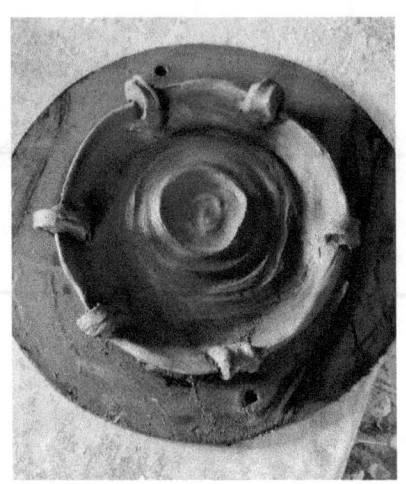

The Salsa and Corn Chip dish designed in the style of a Hat is a representation of the Sun going in a Circular motion for the Native American crop harvest of Corn. It also represents the Circle of the Dance in Celebration of the harvest.

Sundial Disk

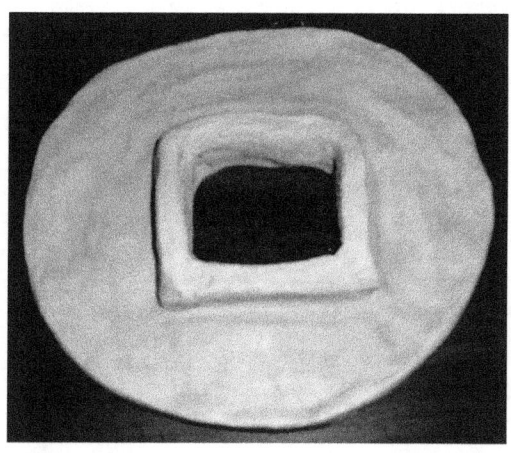

The Sundial Disk is used by many Cultures found around the world. At different degrees of Sun Rays, it can tell people what time of day it is by casting a Shadow by the position of the sun.

There are many different styles produced by the Ancient people of various cultures. Some of these areas include Egypt, Mexico, China, Scotland and Ireland.

Pacific Starfish

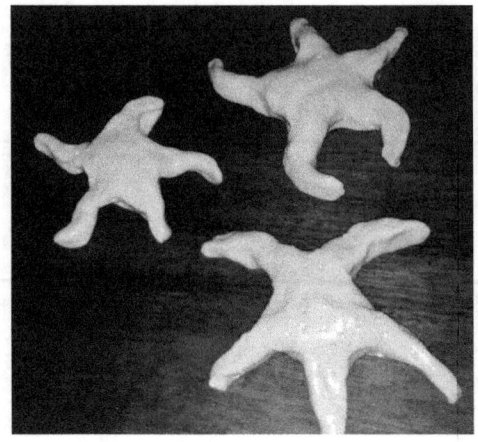

Starfish are found throughout the Coastal regions of the Pacific Ocean.

Literary Published Works

Peggy Leyva Conley

Books

The Potter and Sculptress
Clay/Ceramic Wheel Throwing/Hand Designs – Published 2016

Landscape Paintings and Haiku Poetry
Coastlines-Mountains-Terrain – Published 2016

Vibrant Flowers and Garden
Painting-Drawings – Published 2016

Drawing and Paintings
Poetry – Published 2016

Nature Calling
Photography-Poetry – Published 2016

Winter Season with Nature – Landscape Scenes
Poetry and Photography - Published 2016

Life in the Country – White Cotton Sheets
Poetry and Photography – Published 2016

At the Heart of Aromatherapy – Nature Botanicals
Herbs – Soaps – Oils – Fragrance – Published 2016

The Transcendental Zen Garden
Poetry and Photography – Published 2016

Poetic Inspirations
Poetry and Photography – Published 2016

Discography - Music

Passages of Time

(Classical: Film Music) - Released 2010

Canterbury Manor
(Classical: Chamber Music) – Released 2013

Ancient Garden of Knowledge
(Classical: Orchestral) – Released 2013

Midnight Telephone Blues
(Blues: Delta Style) - Released 2013

In the Face of Blues
(Acoustic Blues) – Released 2013

Mountain Blues
(Acoustic Blues) – Released 2013

Available on International Distribution

www.ingramcontent.com/pod-product-compliance
Lightning Source LLC
Chambersburg PA
CBHW080639190526
45169CB00009B/3428